My Name Starts With M

For my marvelous granddaughters, Madison, Mollie, and Myla, I make this book.

By Larry Hayes

Featuring the art of Airlie Anderson

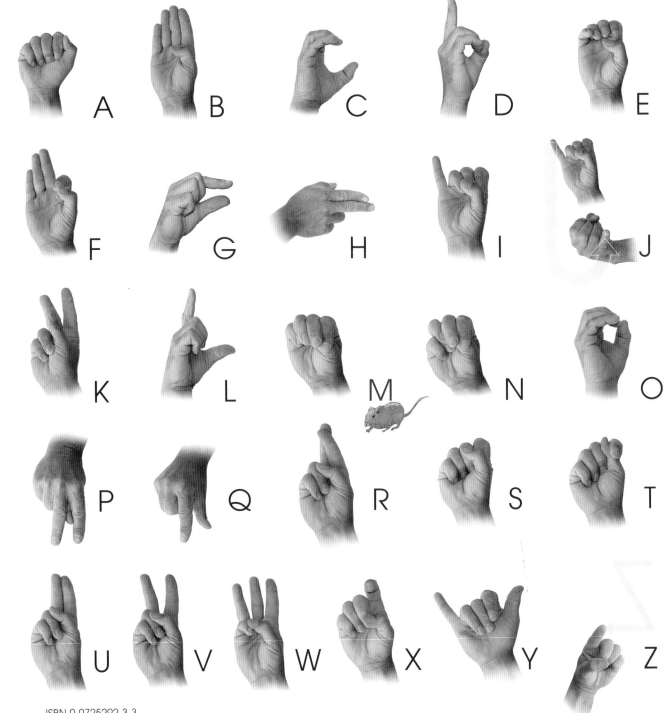

ISBN 0-9725292-3-3

2

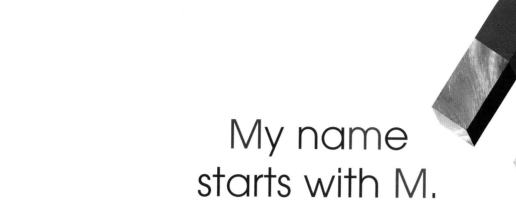

My name starts with M.

Mommy and Daddy
say
my name is special.

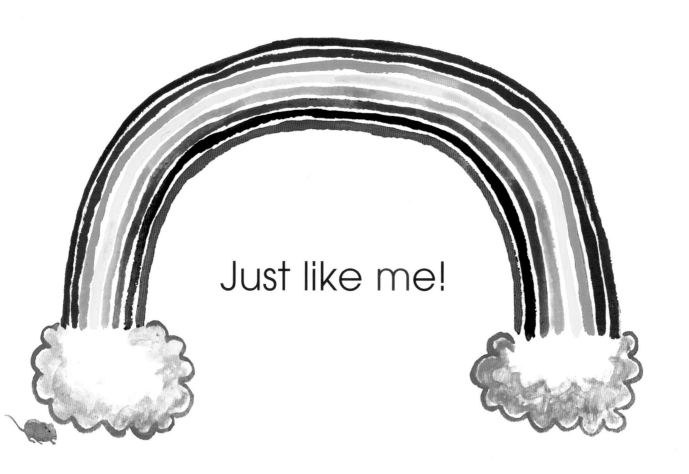

Just like me!

Some m's are small
and some M's are big.
See the animals and
insects starting with small m.

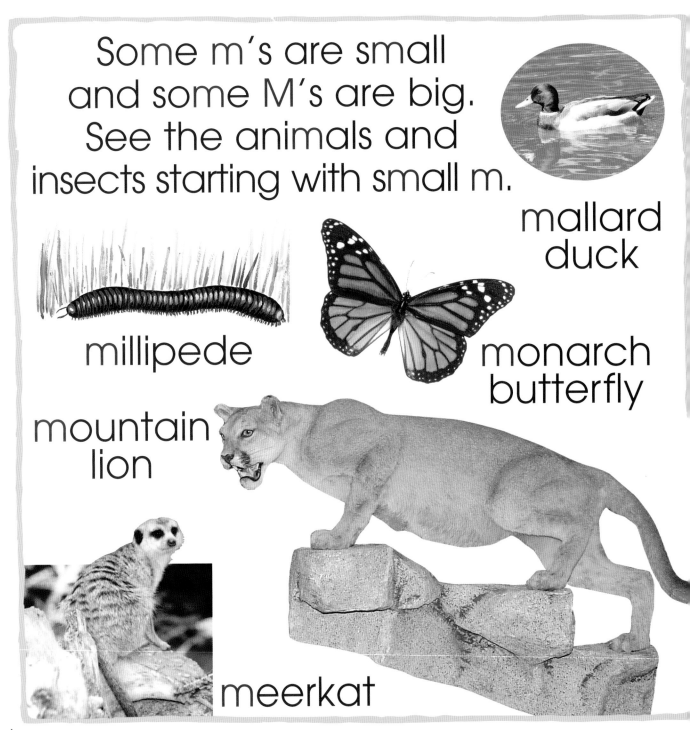

mallard
duck

millipede

monarch
butterfly

mountain
lion

meerkat

monkeys

miniature
horse

macaw

moth

Big M is the letter
that begins the
names of these
four friends:

Madison Max Myla Mollie

Things that I see begin
with small m.

magnet

magnifying
glass

mailboxes

manicure

mammoth

marriage

medal

mermaids

marigolds

moon

mime

There are magnificent places in the world starting with big M.

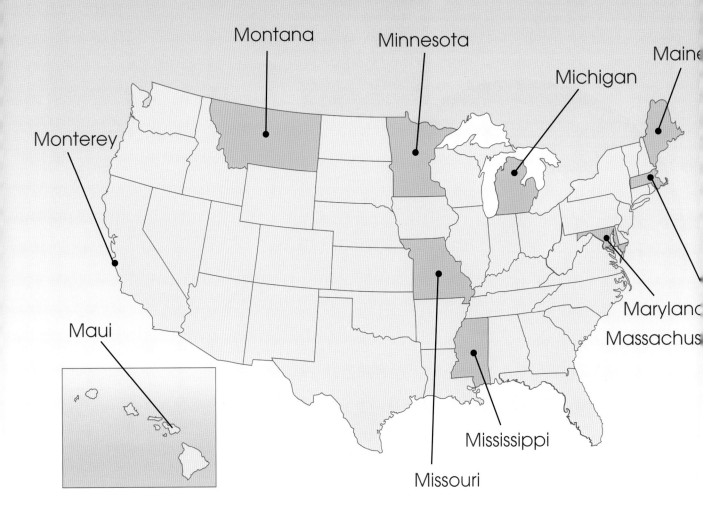

Montana
Minnesota
Michigan
Maine
Monterey
Maui
Maryland
Massachus
Mississippi
Missouri

Map of the United States

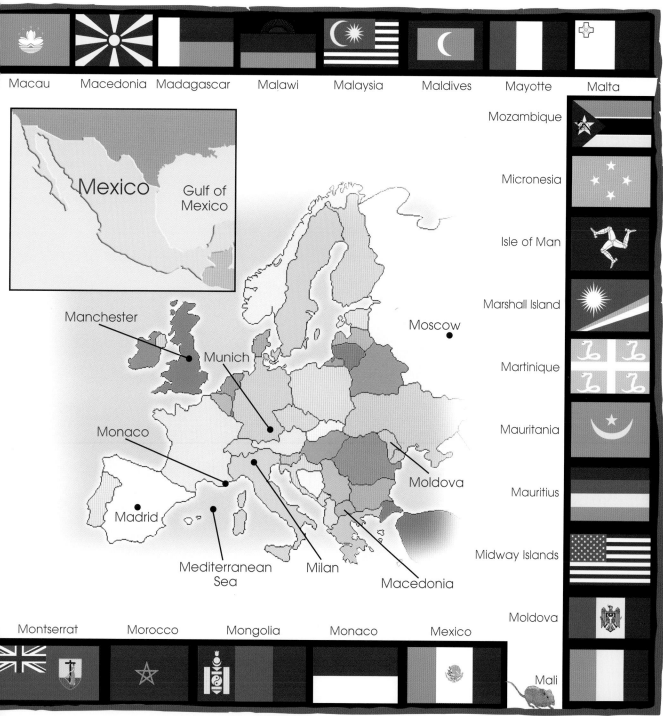

Macau   Macedonia   Madagascar   Malawi   Malaysia   Maldives   Mayotte   Malta

Mozambique

Micronesia

Isle of Man

Marshall Island

Martinique

Mauritania

Mauritius

Midway Islands

Moldova

Mexico

Gulf of
Mexico

Manchester

Munich

Moscow

Monaco

Moldova

Madrid

Mediterranean
Sea

Milan

Macedonia

Montserrat   Morocco   Mongolia   Monaco   Mexico

Mali

Count the
M's you
see here.

Many mice making music march merrily in the meadow by the mountain in the moonlight at midnight.

I munch on foods
that start with m.
Mmmmmm!

meatballs

muffin

mushrooms

melons

meat

milk

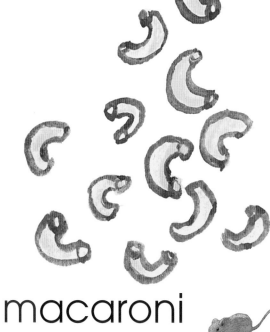

macaroni

Much marine life starts with m.

manatee

minnows

moray eel

A museum is a place where you may see mighty mammals.

mammoth

Touch the M's
and trace
their shapes.

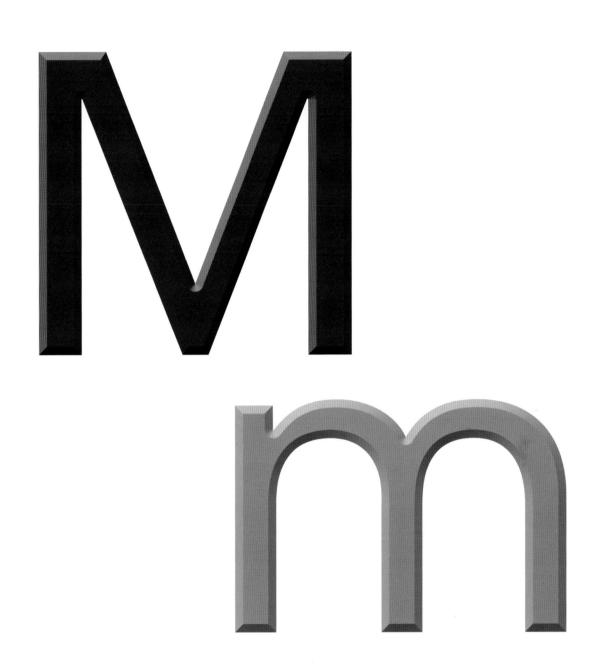

Can you
find the things
starting with M on
these pages?

The sky and space are full of words with M.

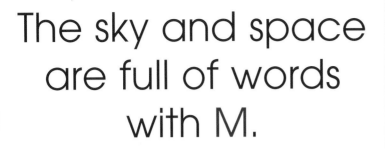

men on the moon

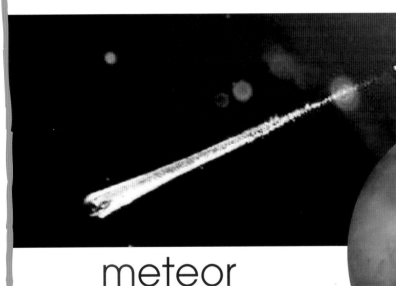

meteor

Mars

Milky Way

meteor shower

Even things we do start with M.

move

martial arts

multiply
in
math

Mexican
dance

Mommy and Daddy
are right.
My name is
special!

It starts with

How many mice did you see in this book?

Did you find these M objects on pages 24 and 25?

moose   moon
moat   mare
mouse   monster
merry-go-round mouse's tail
map
moth
mask
music

Most importantly, did you have fun reading?

IDEAS & SUGGESTIONS:
If not a library copy, this book can be personalized by having the child write his or
her name on page 3 and by pasting a photo of the child under the rainbow on
page 5. You can change the title to just about anything you desire, using your
own calligraphy or clear stickers. For example, the title can become My Last
Name Starts With, My School's Name Starts With, My Doctor's Name Starts With,
My Hometown's Name Starts With, and so forth. A sticker sheet is available with
some of these options, or you may print your own Avery 1/2" labels to insert on
the four pages of the book where the text appears.

Mother's
"My ⌄ Name Starts With M"

Sticker sheets are available at the store where this book was purchased, or visit
our website at www.MyNameStartsWith.com

In an emergency dial 911 and help will be sent.

(A public service page)

MyName Starts With

Larry Hayes, Inspire Publications SAN: 2 5 5 -1 2 2 5
13229 Middle Canyon Road
Carmel Valley, CA 93924
831-917-6059 or toll free: 877-820-1473

Illustrations by Airlie Anderson
Book Design by Jenny Q. Sandrof of Blue Heron Design Group

Credits

Page 26 Space photos: NASA.
Page 27 "move": USN
Other photos by Larry Hayes

Find us on the World Wide Web at
www.MyNameStartsWith.com

ISBN 0-9725292-3-3

Be merry and have
many magical memories